Workbook for
# The Heart of Anger

# Workbook for

## The Heart of Anger

Practical Help for the Prevention
and Cure of Anger in Children

# Lou Priolo and Amy Baker

CALVARY PRESS • 2003 • AMITYVILLE, NY

CALVARY PRESS PUBLISHING
Post Office Box 805
Amityville, NY  11701
1-800-789-8175
www.calvarypress.com

Priolo, Lou, and Amy Baker
    Workbook for The Heart of Anger / by Lou Priolo and Amy Baker.
    ISBN 1-879737-51-5
Suggested subject headings:
1. Christian living—anger—counseling literature
2. Religion—Christian literature—counseling literature
3. The Bible—anger—teaching literature.
I. Title

10 9 8 7 6 5 4 3 2 1

# Contents

# Introduction

There is no doubt that we live in an angry age. Each day as we turn on the radio, TV, or log onto the internet, we see and hear the angry faces of our age. We might even be quick to think, "Praise God, I'm a Christian and am immune to these things," but this is wishful thinking. If the truth be told, we would quickly admit that all families and individuals, Christian and non-Christian, struggle with the issue of anger. Indeed, of all the emotions identified in Scripture, anger is addressed the most.

But not all anger is sinful. "God is angry with the wicked every day" (Psalm 7:11 KJV). The questions we ask ourselves when we become angry will help determine not only whether our anger is righteous or sinful, but also what it is in our hearts that disposes us to get angry.

"What happened that provoked me to anger?"

"What did I say or do when I became angry?"

"What was it that I really wanted when I became angry?

"Am I angry because I didn't get what I wanted or because God didn't get what He wanted?"

"How could I have responded more biblically to the provocation?"

"What does God expect me to do the next time I am provoked to anger?"

Our modern culture is awash with pop-psychology and with new "gurus" telling us how to raise our children and manage our relationships. But the wisdom of the world can never be the barometer of how we respond to life. That is why I originally wrote *The Heart of Anger*. There was a need to get to "the heart of the matter." So I went to the ultimate instruction book on relationships and behavior: the Bible. The fact that *The Heart of Anger* speaks initially to children should not mislead you. The same kinds of desire that produce anger in children (love of pleasure, love of approval, covetousness, etc.) reside in our own hearts as well. This is what I tried to address in the book.

Each chapter of this workbook contains two sets of questions. First are the study questions (designed to help you get the most out of reading *The Heart of*

*Anger*). The next set is the application questions (designed to help you relate what you have read to your life and the lives of your children). By answering these questions, you may be led to new insights about what God expects from you as a Christian parent. May God bless you as you direct the truth of Scripture from your heart to the hearts of your children.

I would like to take this opportunity to thank my coauthor, Amy Baker, who actually spent many more hours working on this project than I, and Fern Gregory, who carefully proofread the text.

Lou Priolo

NOTE: All biblical references in this workbook are from the New American Standard Bible unless otherwise noted.

Workbook for
# The Heart of Anger

# Chapter 1
## Study Questions

1. What does James 1:5 promise God will provide that parents need for child raising?

2. What does 2 Peter 1:3 promise God will provide that parents need for child raising?

3. What *two* things does Philippians 2:13 promise God will provide that parents need for child raising?

4. According to Ephesians 6:4, how do parents show love (obedience) to God and to their children?

5. When God gives a biblical mandate, what does He also provide?

6. Why is it important to initially work with parents when children are having problems?

7. How could one hour of the counselor's good influence each week be negated?

8. What happens to a person who continually yields a member of his body to a particular sin?

9. What are some sins which God uses as labels for those enslaved to those sins?

10. Give examples of categories of people in whom it is possible to see rebellion. Against whom/what might these people rebel?

11. How does being hurt produce bitterness?

12. How should one handle being hurt?

13. How does anger become characterological?

14. Why is stubbornness identified as idolatry?

15. The characteristics of a rebel are essentially the same as those of what other type of person?

16. What is a child-centered home?

17. What indiscretions are children in a child-centered home allowed to commit?

18. What might a child from a child-centered home believe about society when he or she grows up?

19. Why does the husband/wife relationship take precedence over the parent/child relationship?

20. What is the main feature of a God-centered home?

21. What are some evidences that a home is God-centered, not child-centered?

*One flesh*

*Not one flesh*

# Chapter 1
# Application Questions

1. On a scale of 1 (best) to 4 (worst), rate yourself on whether you have the characteristics of a fool.

> 1 = Rarely true of me.
> 2 = Sometimes true of me.
> 3 = Often true of me.
> 4 = Regularly true of me.

| | |
|---|---|
| a. He despises wisdom and instruction. | 1 2 3 4 |
| b. He hates knowledge. | 1 2 3 4 |
| c. He enjoys devising mischief. | 1 2 3 4 |
| d. He is quick to anger. | 1 2 3 4 |
| e. He is right in his own eyes. | 1 2 3 4 |
| f. He hates to depart from evil. | 1 2 3 4 |
| g. He is deceitful. | 1 2 3 4 |
| h. He is arrogant and careless. | 1 2 3 4 |
| i. He rejects instruction from authority. | 1 2 3 4 |
| j. He despises authority. | 1 2 3 4 |
| k. He does not respond well to correction. | 1 2 3 4 |
| l. He does not understand wisdom. | 1 2 3 4 |
| m. He has a worldly (carnal) focus (value system). | 1 2 3 4 |
| n. He grieves those in authority. | 1 2 3 4 |
| o. He does not consider discussing any viewpoint but his own. | 1 2 3 4 |
| p. He provokes others to strife and anger by the things he says. | 1 2 3 4 |
| q. He has a smart mouth that gets him into trouble. | 1 2 3 4 |
| r. He is quarrelsome. | 1 2 3 4 |
| s. He is a spendthrift. | 1 2 3 4 |
| t. He repeats his folly. | 1 2 3 4 |
| u. He trusts in his own thinking. | 1 2 3 4 |
| v. He cannot resolve conflicts. | 1 2 3 4 |
| w. He gives full vent to his anger. | 1 2 3 4 |

2. Draw a picture of the way you believe each of your children views your home (child-centered, parent-centered, dad-centered, mom-centered, partly child-centered, God-centered).

3. Rate each child in your home on the following scale.

> **1** = Rarely true of child.
> **2** = Sometimes true of child.
> **3** = Often true of child.
> **4** = Regularly true of child.

| | |
|---|---|
| a. Knows the joy of serving others. | 1 2 3 4 |
| b. Cheerfully obeys parents the first time. | 1 2 3 4 |
| c. Does not interrupt parents who are speaking to each other. | 1 2 3 4 |
| d. Does not manipulate others. | 1 2 3 4 |
| e. Knows that he/she is not always going to get his/her own way. | 1 2 3 4 |
| f. Works his/her schedule around his/her parents' schedule. | 1 2 3 4 |
| g. Has input into family decisions but not necessarily an equal vote. | 1 2 3 4 |
| h. Understands that God has given his/her parents responsibilities in addition to meeting his/her needs. | 1 2 3 4 |
| i. Suffers the natural consequences of his/her sinful and irresponsible behavior. | 1 2 3 4 |
| j. Doesn't speak to parents as though they are peers but honors them as spiritual authorities. | 1 2 3 4 |
| k. Esteems others as more important than himself / herself. | 1 2 3 4 |
| l. Fulfills various household responsibilities (chores). | 1 2 3 4 |
| m. Protects himself / herself from bad influences. | 1 2 3 4 |
| n. Does not divide parents on disciplinary issues. | 1 2 3 4 |
| o. Is not more intimate with either parent than the parents are with each other. | 1 2 3 4 |

4. Ask someone who is godly, truthful, and unbiased to rate you on question 1. (Be prepared to handle the fact that this person may point out faults you would rather not face.)

# Chapter 2
## Study Questions

1. Are parents responsible for a child's anger problem? Explain.

2. How does lack of marital harmony between husband and wife provoke children to anger?

3. Why would it be harmful for children to see themselves as equal to their parents?

4. What are some ways sinful anger might be displayed in a home?

5. What view of problems is taught by a parent who models sinful anger?

6. How does disciplining in anger provoke children?

7. What should be the parents' emphasis in discipline?
   What should it not be?

8. What is scolding?

9. Is it wrong to talk to a child when there has been wrongdoing?
   Why or why not?

10. What indicators might show that a parent has crossed the line from
    biblical reproof to scolding?

11. In what ways might inconsistent discipline be displayed?

12. Why might parents be inconsistent?

13. In what areas might parents have double standards?

14. Define legalism.

15. What is "the law of the house"?

16. What is the difference between biblically-directed rules and biblically-derived rules?

17. Why may children appeal biblically-derived rules but not biblically-directed rules?

18. What attitude might children develop if parents do not admit when they are wrong?

19. What are four steps to follow in asking forgiveness?

20. Write out how a parent who has snapped at his/her child in anger when the child disobeyed should seek forgiveness.

21. What is probably the most effective safeguard against being a parent who constantly finds fault?

22. To avoid becoming fault-finding parents, should parents avoid pointing out sinful behavior in their child? Why or why not? What should they do?

23. What is wrong with reversing God-given roles?

24. What might not listening to the child's opinion or side of the story communicate to the child?

25. What are forward and backward comparisons?

26. What kind of comparisons should not be made? What kind of comparisons are appropriate?

27. What will be the result if parents do not make time to talk to their children?

28. What kinds of things might cause parents to not take time to talk with their children?

29. What two components are part of an accurate self-perception?

30. How does praise help children?

31. With what emotions may a child struggle if parents fail to keep promises?

32. When a parent needs to break a commitment, what should the parent do? When a parent has broken a commitment, what should the parent do?

33. What is the biblical way to break a contract?

34. How may a child begin to view a parent who has broken many promises?

35. What disciplinary principle is derived from Matthew 18:15?

36. What does it mean to give a child too much freedom?

37. Why would it be right for a child who is not disciplined to conclude that he/she is not loved?

38. How is faithfulness demonstrated?

39. What are some reasons for parents not giving their children enough freedom?

40. Why should a parent not make fun of a child's intelligence, athletic abilities, physical features, or motor coordination?

41. Why should a parent not make fun of things that are sinful?

42. What causes a parent to physically abuse a child?

43. What are some unbiblical motivations for discipline which may lead to physical abuse?

44. What biblical criteria must be met if one is to use "name-calling?"

45. List several names that do not meet biblical criteria?

46. What should be more important than achievement or perfection?

47. In order to avoid favoritism, should all children be treated the same? Why or why not?

48. How can parents treat children as individuals without showing favoritism?

49. Why will the world's methods of child training not work?

50. What should parents who have been provoking their children to anger do?

# Chapter 2
## Application Questions

1. List the rules in your home. Beside each, indicate which are biblically-directed and which are biblically-derived.

2. List the biblical principles on which your biblically-derived rules are based.

3. Ask your children to tell you which rules in your house are biblically-directed and which are biblically-derived.

4. When would your children say was the last time you admitted you were wrong and sought forgiveness? How consistently would they say you seek forgiveness?

5. What things in your life might prevent you from making time to talk with your children?

6. What, if anything, does this say about your priorities?

7. Rate yourself on each of 25 characteristics which provoke children to anger. On the blank beside each statement, write the number that best describes what you believe to be true of your family situation.

    **1** = Hardly ever
    **2** = Occasionally
    **3** = Frequently
    **4** = Almost always

| | |
|---|---|
| a. I lack marital harmony. | 1 2 3 4 |
| b. I have a child-centered home. | 1 2 3 4 |
| c. I model sinful anger. | 1 2 3 4 |
| d. I consistently discipline in anger. | 1 2 3 4 |
| e. I scold. | 1 2 3 4 |
| f. I am inconsistent in discipline. | 1 2 3 4 |
| g. I have double standards. | 1 2 3 4 |
| h. I am legalistic. | 1 2 3 4 |
| i. I do not admit when I am wrong. | 1 2 3 4 |
| j. I continually find fault. | 1 2 3 4 |
| k. I reverse God-given roles. | 1 2 3 4 |
| l. I do not listen to my child's opinion or my child's side of the story. | 1 2 3 4 |
| m. I compare my child with others. | 1 2 3 4 |
| n. I do not have time to talk with my child. | 1 2 3 4 |
| o. I do not praise my child. | 1 2 3 4 |

p. I fail to keep promises to my child.     1 2 3 4

q. I chastise my child in front of others.    1 2 3 4

r. I give my child too much freedom.     1 2 3 4

s. I do not give my child enough freedom.   1 2 3 4

t. I make fun of my child.        1 2 3 4

u. I abuse my child physically.      1 2 3 4

v. I call my child names.        1 2 3 4

w. I have unrealistic expectations for my child.  1 2 3 4

x. I show favoritism.         1 2 3 4

y. I use child-training methods that are inconsistent with God's word. 1 2 3 4

8. For any characteristic on which you gave yourself a 3 or a 4, give *two* examples of how you see this to be true in your life.

9. For each characteristic on which you gave yourself a 3 or a 4, list specific steps you will implement in order to change.

10. For each characteristic on which you gave yourself a 3 or a 4, seek forgiveness from God, your child, and any appropriate others.

11. Ask your spouse to fill out the rating scale for you. Discuss the answers.

12. Ask someone who is godly, truthful, and unbiased to rate you on these characteristics. (Be prepared to handle the fact that this person may point out faults you would rather not face.)

# Chapter 3
## Study Questions

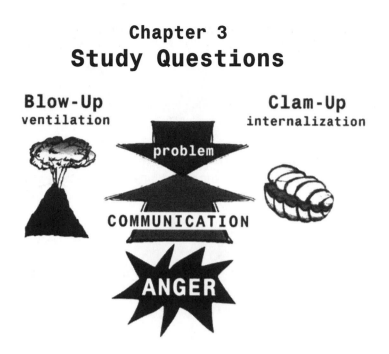

**Blow-Up**
ventilation

**Clam-Up**
internalization

problem

COMMUNICATION

ANGER

1. What does it mean to "internalize" anger?

2. What does it mean to "ventilate" anger?

3. What does God want us to destroy with anger?

4. What will usually be necessary to solve problems biblically?

5. What three elements make up communication?

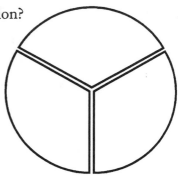

6. Why is it so important to think about
   and plan what to say when angry?

7. Give biblical evidence that God believes tone of voice is important.

8. What does nonverbal communication include?

9. Underline the facial expression given in each of the following verses
   and tell what attitude is portrayed.

   Psalm 10:4 The wicked, in the haughtiness of his countenance, does not seek
   Him. All his thoughts are, "There is no God."

   Genesis 4:5 But for Cain and for his offering He had no regard. So Cain
   became very angry and his countenance fell.

   Daniel 5:5-6 ⁵Suddenly the fingers of a man's hand emerged and began writing opposite the lampstand on the plaster of the wall of the king's palace, and
   the king saw the back of the hand that did the writing. ⁶Then the king's face
   grew pale, and his thoughts alarmed him; and his hip joints went slack, and
   his knees began knocking together.

Proverbs 6:25 Do not desire her beauty in your heart, Nor let her catch you with her eyelids.

Proverbs 30:17 The eye that mocks a father, And scorns a mother, The ravens of the valley will pick it out, And the young eagles will eat it.

Ezra 9:6-7 6And I said, "O my God, I am ashamed and embarrassed to lift up my face to Thee, my God, for our iniquities have risen above our heads, and our guilt has grown even to the heavens. 7"Since the days of our fathers to this day we have been in great guilt, and on account of our iniquities we, our kings and our priests have been given into the hand of the kings of the lands, to the sword, to captivity, and to plunder and to open shame, as it is this day.

Ecclesiastes 8:1 Who is like the wise man and who knows the interpretation of a matter? A man's wisdom illumines him and causes his stern face to beam.

Deuteronomy 31:17 "Then My anger will be kindled against them in that day, and I will forsake them and hide My face from them, and they shall be consumed, and many evils and troubles shall come upon them; so that they will say in that day, 'Is it not because our God is not among us that these evils have come upon us?'

Numbers 6:25 The Lord make His face shine on you, And be gracious to you.

1 Samuel 1:18 And she said, "Let your maidservant find favor in your sight." So the woman went her way and ate, and her face was no longer sad.

Job 16:16 "My face is flushed from weeping, And deep darkness is on my eyelids."

Job 41:14 "Who can open the doors of his face? Around his teeth there is terror."

Psalm 69:7 Because for Thy sake I have borne reproach; Dishonor has covered my face.

Proverbs 7:13 So she seizes him and kisses him, And with a brazen face she says to him:

Proverbs 15:13 A joyful heart makes a cheerful face, But when the heart is sad, the spirit is broken.

Proverbs 21:29 A wicked man shows a bold face, But as for the upright, he makes his way sure.

Deuteronomy 7:16 "And you shall consume all the peoples whom the Lord your God will deliver to you; your eye shall not pity them, neither shall you serve their gods, for that would be a snare to you.

Deuteronomy 15:9 "Beware, lest there is a base thought in your heart, saying, 'The seventh year, the year of remission, is near,' and your eye is hostile toward your poor brother, and you give him nothing; then he may cry to the Lord against you, and it will be a sin in you."

Job 17:7 "My eye has also grown dim because of grief, And all my members are as a shadow."

Psalm 92:11 And my eye has looked exultantly upon my foes, My ears hear of the evildoers who rise up against me.

Matthew 20:15 'Is it not lawful for me to do what I wish with what is my own? Or is your eye envious because I am generous?'

10. Why is changing facial expressions probably the most difficult aspect of communication to correct?

# Chapter 3
# Application Questions

1. What *general* pattern do you tend to follow when you handle problems sinfully? (Blow up, clam up, blow up and then clam up, clam up and then blow up.)

2. What are the *specific* ways these tendencies are displayed? (I walk away; I use sarcasm; I raise my voice; I give the person at whom I am angry "the cold shoulder," etc.)

3. What *specific* things have you been doing to put off sinful anger and put on using that energy to solve problems?

4. Think about the last upset you had. Write out specifically how you handled it. Include the words you said, the tones you used, and what your nonverbal actions were. Are there any aspects of the upset you wish you had handled differently? If so, write out specifically the words, tones, and nonverbal actions which would have been more pleasing to God.

# Chapter 4
## Study Questions

1. What is the first rule for disciplining children?

2. What is the difference between training and teaching?

3. Identify whether each of the following statements refers to teaching or to training.

   It causes another to do.
   It causes another to know.
   It fills the mind.
   It gives knowledge.
   It shapes habits.
   It gives skill.
   It enables a child to use what is already in his/her possession.
   It informs the child of something he/she did not have before.

4. How is training possible before there has been teaching?

5. What is a habit?

6. What does the word *discipline* mean?

7. Why is just asking forgiveness not sufficient in proper discipline?

# Chapter 4
# Application Questions

1. How would you rate yourself on personal self-discipline? Consider each of the following areas. Use the following rating scale.

> 1 = Self-discipline in this area is a habit.
> 2 = There has been consistent growth in this area of self-discipline.
> 3 = Growth in this area has been sporadic and irregular.
> 4 = There is little to no self-discipline in this area. Basically, I live by my feelings when it comes to this area.

| | |
|---|---|
| Eating | 1 2 3 4 |
| Use of time | 1 2 3 4 |
| Television watching | 1 2 3 4 |
| Memorization | 1 2 3 4 |
| Bible study | 1 2 3 4 |
| Use of finances | 1 2 3 4 |
| Exercise | 1 2 3 4 |
| Completing household chores | 1 2 3 4 |
| Getting up on time | 1 2 3 4 |
| Going to bed on time | 1 2 3 4 |
| Controlling my thinking | 1 2 3 4 |
| Work habits | 1 2 3 4 |
| Speech | 1 2 3 4 |
| Reading material | 1 2 3 4 |
| Use of free time | 1 2 3 4 |
| Other areas (please list) | 1 2 3 4 |

2. What would you have a child do in each of the following situations to require him / her to practice the biblical alternative?

The child has been disrespectful.

The child has stolen.

The child is inattentive.

The child is ungrateful.

The child has tattled.

The child has lied.

The child is unkind.

The child has whined.

The child has been rude.

The child is shy.

The child interrupts.

The child blame shifts.

The child is argumentative.

The child fights with siblings.

The child is vindictive.

# Chapter 5
## Study Questions

1. What are some common violations of biblical communication?

2. Why should biblical terminology be used in confession?

3. Why is saying "I'm sorry" not as effective as saying, "Will you forgive me?"

4. What three aspects should be included in correcting wrong communication?

5. How should you think about the fact that doing this will take more time?

# Chapter 5
# Application Questions

1. Rate yourself on your use of sinful forms of communication using the following scale.

    1 = Hardly ever
    2 = Occasionally
    3 = Frequently
    4 = Almost always

    | | |
    |---|---|
    | a. Ungracious communication | 1 2 3 4 |
    | b. Disrespect | 1 2 3 4 |
    | c. Interruption | 1 2 3 4 |
    | d. Not communicating | 1 2 3 4 |
    | e. Name-calling | 1 2 3 4 |
    | f. Judging motives | 1 2 3 4 |
    | g. Raising the voice | 1 2 3 4 |
    | h. Rolling the eyes | 1 2 3 4 |
    | i. Manipulation | 1 2 3 4 |
    | j. Sulking/Pouting | 1 2 3 4 |
    | k. Angry countenance | 1 2 3 4 |
    | l. Inattentiveness | 1 2 3 4 |

2. What specific changes do you need to make (or are you making) in any sinful forms of communication being used?

3. Now rate your children, using the same scale on their use of sinful forms of communication. (You may want to make a separate list for each child.)

4. What do you do to correct each sinful form of communication in the children you listed? How consistent are you in doing this?

5. Explain how you might correct the following:

Your six-year-old daughter interrupts you while you are talking to an adult at church.

Your 14-year-old son is watching TV and makes no response when you walk into the room and tell him it is time to turn it off and come to dinner.

Your four-year-old son stomps off complaining when told to go pick up his toys.

Your 17-year-old daughter rolls her eyes when you ask her if she had a good day at school.

Your eight-year-old son angrily tells you to get out of *his* room.

Your 10-year-old daughter mocks your spouse.

# Chapter 6
## Study Questions

1. List five uses of the anger journal.

2. What four questions does a child answer in keeping an anger journal?

3. What two purposes are served by identifying the circumstances which provoked the anger?

4. How do we know that not all anger is sinful?

5. Identify whether each of the following is sinful anger or could be righteous anger and why?

   I did not get to go to my friend's house when I wanted to go.

   I have learned that my daughter is sexually active.

   I watched a child show disrespect to her mother.

   I did not get to watch my favorite TV program because of my child's disobedience.

6. How could anger at a child for being disobedient be both sinful and righteous?

7. Why is it important to have a child record the details of an angry response?

8. Match the following actions or words with the appropriate verse on this and the following page. (Some verses will be used more than once.)

| | | | |
|---|---|---|---|
| _____ Arguing | _____ Mocking |
| _____ Bitter | _____ Proud |
| _____ Boasting | _____ Quarrelsome |
| _____ Clamor | _____ Selfish |
| _____ Complaining | _____ Slanderers |
| _____ Cursing | _____ Striker |
| _____ Deceitful | _____ Strife |
| _____ Disobedient | _____ Uncontrolled |
| _____ Gossip | _____ Unforgiving |
| _____ Harsh | _____ Ungrateful |
| _____ Hateful | _____ Unkind |
| _____ Hurtful | _____ Unloving |
| _____ Impatient | _____ Unmerciful |
| _____ Insolent | _____ Vengeful |
| _____ Intolerant | _____ Vulgarity |
| _____ Malice | _____ Wrath |

a. A gentle answer turns away wrath, but a harsh word stirs up anger. (Proverbs 15:1)

b. All who hate me whisper together against me: against me they devise my hurt. (Psalm 41:7)

c. Do everything without complaining or arguing. (Philippians 2:14, NIV)

d. Without understanding, untrustworthy, unloving, unmerciful. (Romans 1:31)

e. Let all bitterness and wrath and anger and clamor and slander be put away from you, along with all malice. (Ephesians 4:31)

f. But now you must rid yourselves of all such things as these: anger, rage, malice, slander, and filthy language from your lips. (Colossians 3:8, NIV)

g. And be kind to one another, tender-hearted, forgiving each other, just as God in Christ also has forgiven you (Ephesians 4:32)

h. Being filled with all unrighteousness, wickedness, greed, evil; full of envy, murder, strife, deceit, malice; they are gossips. (Romans 1:29)

i. For men will be lovers of self, lovers of money, boastful, arrogant, revilers, disobedient to parents, ungrateful, unholy. (2 Timothy 3:2)

j. Idolatry, witchcraft, hatred, variance, emulations, wrath, strife, seditions, heresies. (Galatians 5:20, KJV)

k. From the same mouth come both blessing and cursing. My brethren, these things ought not to be this way. (James 3:10)

l. Do not take revenge, my friends, but leave room for God's wrath, for it is written: "It is mine to avenge; I will repay," says the Lord (Romans 12:19, NIV)

m. With all humility and gentleness, with patience, showing forbearance to one another in love. (Ephesians 4:2)

n. Slanderers, haters of God, insolent, arrogant, boastful, inventors of evil, disobedient to parents. (Romans 1:30)

o. If you are wise, your wisdom will reward you; if you are a mocker, you alone will suffer." (Proverbs 9:12, NIV)

p. Not given to wine, no striker, not greedy of filthy lucre; but patient, not a brawler, not covetous. (1 Timothy 3:3, KJV)

q. Unloving, irreconcilable, malicious gossips, without self-control, brutal, haters of good. (2 Timothy 3:3)

9. Answer questions 3 and 4 on the anger journal for each of the following situations. (List two or three biblical alternative responses for each.)

When child does not get his mother's attention immediately, child manipulates to get attention by claiming a need to go to the bathroom.

Child wants to stop at McDonald's and sulks by refusing to talk to the family when denied.

Child kicked mom when told by mom to move.

Child made fun of the teacher when the teacher told the class to pay attention.

Child argues with mother when told to get ready for bed.

10. Why should parents guard against viewing the materials in this book as "behavior modification" or "cognitive therapy techniques"?

# Chapter 6
# Application Questions

1. Do an anger journal for yourself for two weeks.

2. Keep a record of changes you make to please God as a result of using the anger journal.

3. Do an anger journal with each of your children for two weeks (unpacking his or her angry responses).

4. Review each child's anger journal. Try to identify any "common denominators" (common trigger issues) for each one. For some possible categories, please refer to the classifications and Scripture passages on pages 45 and 46 (question 8 of the Study Questions for Chapter Six).

---

## Is Your Anger Righteous or Sinful?

| Righteous Anger | Sinful Anger |
| --- | --- |
| When God doesn't get what He wants. | When I don't get what I want. |
| Motivated by a sincere love for God. | Motivated by a love of some idolatrous desire. |
| God's will is violated. | My will is violated. |
| *Christ is Lord of my life.* | *I am the lord of my life.* |
| "Be angry, and do not sin." (Eph. 4:26) | "What is the source of quarrels and conflicts among you? Is not the source your pleasures that wage war in your members?" (James 4:1) |

---

# Chapter 7
## Study Questions

1. Feelings are by-products of what?

The Lips, Mouth, and Tongue

2. What is the heart?

3. Since only God can know the heart, how can parents learn what is going on in a child's heart?

4. Why is it not enough to merely teach your child to behave as a Christian?

5. What is the purpose of the heart journal?

6. List five things the heart journal can do to help you train your child.

7. What two purposes are served by asking a child to describe what provoked his/her anger?

8. After each of the following verses, write out what we learn about thinking.

   2 Corinthians 10:5 We demolish arguments and every pretension that sets itself up against the knowledge of God, and we take captive every thought to make it obedient to Christ. (NIV)

   Deuteronomy 15:9 "Be careful not to harbor this wicked thought: 'The seventh year, the year for canceling debts, is near,' so that you do not show ill will toward your needy brother and give him nothing. He may then appeal to the LORD against you, and you will be found guilty of sin." (NIV)

   Psalm 15:2 He whose walk is blameless and who does what is righteous, who speaks the truth from his heart. (NIV)

Isaiah 55:7 Let the wicked forsake his way and the evil man his thoughts. Let him turn to the Lord, and he will have mercy on him, and to our God, for he will freely pardon. (NIV)

Matthew 15:19 For out of the heart come evil thoughts, murder, adultery, sexual immorality, theft, false testimony, slander. (NIV)

Jeremiah 17:9 The heart is deceitful above all things and beyond cure. Who can understand it? (NIV)

9. What things make recognizing wrong motives more difficult?

10. Is there anything wrong, in and of itself, with delighting in another person, a job, a hobby, material things, travel, etc.? Why or why not?

11. Is it possible for things which are not intrinsically sinful as objects of delight to become sinful? How does this happen?

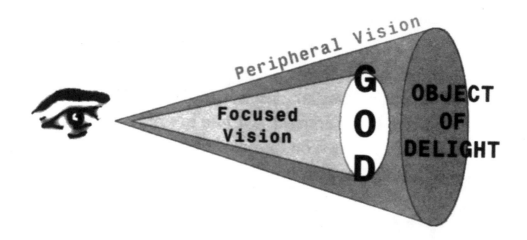

# Chapter 7
# Application Questions

1. Do questions 1 and 2 of the heart journal for two weeks.

2. Answer these "motive identifying" questions. (Answers may overlap.)

   What is it that I believe I cannot be happy without?

   What is it that I crave?

   What is it that I believe I must have?

   About what do I spend most of my spare time thinking?

   What is it that I worry most about losing?

   What is it in which I delight (seek my happiness) the most?

   What is it that I love more than I love God and my neighbor?

3. In what ways do these motives tend to show up in your life?

4. Go through the above questions with each of your children. Think of examples of how you believe these motives might be impacting each one.

# Chapter 8
# Study Questions

1. Why can a problem not be solved biblically until it is diagnosed with biblical terms?

2. List three inherently sinful desires, citing a scripture reference which shows it is sinful.

3. List three desires that are not inherently sinful but which could become sinful.

4. Give examples of how each of the desires you listed above could become sinful.

5. Give a general principle for determining whether or not a desire has become sinful.

6. What is the source of sinful anger?

7. What often demonstrates the presence of an inordinate desire?

8. How can children demonstrate a love of money?

9. How can children demonstrate a love of pleasure?

10. How might children demonstrate a love of approval?

11. How might children demonstrate a love of power or control?

12. What must occur in order for change to be biblical?

13. How does the heart journal train your child to develop a proper motivation?

14. What should be the Christian's first love (greatest desire)?

15. What should a child be trained to ask himself rather than "What do I want to do?"

16. What righteous desire is indicated in each of the following verses?

    2 Corinthians 5:9 So we make it our goal to please Him, whether we are at home in the body or away from it. (NIV)

    Proverbs 4:5 Get wisdom, get understanding; do not forget my words or swerve from them. (NIV)

    Philippians 3:10 I want to know Christ and the power of His resurrection and the fellowship of sharing in His sufferings, becoming like Him in His death, (NIV)

    Psalm 40:8 I desire to do your will, O my God; your law is within my heart." (NIV)

## Chapter 8 Study Questions

Hebrews 13:18 Pray for us. We are sure that we have a clear conscience and desire to live honorably in every way. (NIV)


Psalm 45:7 You have loved righteousness and hated wickedness; Therefore God, Your God, has anointed you with the oil of joy above Your fellows.


Psalm 119:47 I shall delight in Your commandments, which I love.


Proverbs 12:1 Whoever loves discipline loves knowledge, but he who hates reproof is stupid.


Proverbs 22:11 He who loves purity of heart and whose speech is gracious, the king is his friend.

# Chapter 8
# Application Questions

1. List several biblical alternatives for a child to think about for each of the following thoughts.

   "I do not have to obey you."

   "I did not ask to be born."

   "You guys are no fun."

   "I hate this place."

   "I am never going to have to do this once I leave home. Why do I have to do it now?"

   "My parents are too strict."

   "My parents are hypocrites."

   "I hate it when you say that to me."

   "I do not want to do that right now."

2. Keep a heart journal (answering all the questions) for yourself for the next two weeks.

3. Review all of your heart journals, as well as those for each of your children. Try to identify any "common denominators" (common trigger issues) for each one.

4. Keep a record for the next two weeks of ways you grow in pleasing God as a result of using the heart journal. (Record specific acts and thoughts of obedience.)

# Chapter 9
## Study Questions

1. What is manipulation?

2. What are some of the techniques (behaviors) used by those who wish to manipulate?

3. For each of the following manipulative behaviors, list possible desired emotional responses (there may be more than one).

   Withholding affection:

   Pretending not to understand:

   Bringing up issues from the past:

4. For each of the following answers to a manipulative statement, explain why the parental reaction is wrong.

Child: "You never let me go out with my friends."
Parent: "Yes, I do. Just last week, I let you go to Sally's slumber party."

Child: "May I have something to eat?"
Parent: "Not now."
Child: "But, I'm hungry."
Parent: "You ate just two hours ago."

Child: "May I go over to my friend's house?"
Parent: "No. You have homework to do."
Child: (whining)"Why can't I do my homework later?"
Parent: "Because you have a test tomorrow, and I want you to do some extra studying tonight."

Child: "Can I watch TV?"
Parent: "You know the rule; no TV until homework is done and dinner is over."
Child: "Please."
Parent: "No."
Child: "Just this once?"
Parent: "No."
Child: "I promise to not watch it later."
Parent: "Oh, go ahead. But if you don't get your homework done tonight, there'll be no television for you for a week!"

5. How could confronting manipulation in a child be manipulation by the parent?

6. What two antimanipulation devices are suggested in the book? (Explain them in your own words.)

# Chapter 9
# Application Questions

1. Take the manipulation test.

   **5** = Never or hardly ever
   **4** = Seldom
   **3** = Occasionally
   **2** = Frequently
   **1** = Almost always
   **0** = Always

   a. I have to repeat and/or reword instructions
      before my child follows them.                          5 4 3 2 1 0

   b. When I ask my child to do something,
      he asks me, "Why?"                                     5 4 3 2 1 0

   c. I find myself having to justify my decisions to my child.  5 4 3 2 1 0

   d. I have grown weary of certain "topics" which
      seem to be discussed over and over again with my child.  5 4 3 2 1 0

   e. I walk away from discussions with my child feeling guilty.  5 4 3 2 1 0

   f. My child lies to me.                                   5 4 3 2 1 0

   g. My child is disciplined almost entirely by one parent.  5 4 3 2 1 0

   h. I rescind disciplinary actions (or lift restrictions)
      because of appeals by my child.                        5 4 3 2 1 0

   i. I find myself defending my positions to my child.      5 4 3 2 1 0

   j. I get frustrated because my child seems beyond my control.  5 4 3 2 1 0

   k. I get sidetracked by my child's clever distractions
      when I attempt to discipline him.                      5 4 3 2 1 0

   l. My child tries to obligate me to behave a certain way
      by telling me what I should, ought to, or must do
      (other than for biblical reasons).                     5 4 3 2 1 0

   m. When my child wants something from me, he tries to
      motivate me to give it to him without telling me
      directly what he wants.                                5 4 3 2 1 0

   n. My child is able to procrastinate by cleverly using
      numerous stall tactics when I assign him a responsibility.  5 4 3 2 1 0

   o. My child is able to play on my emotions in order to
      get what he wants.                                     5 4 3 2 1 0

p. I hesitate to say "no" to my child out of fear of
what he might do.      5 4 3 2 1 0

q. I am unsuccessful at completing the intended instruction
and discipline of my child due to his unwillingness
to cooperate.      5 4 3 2 1 0

r. My child is so tenacious in wanting his own way that
I either give in to his desires or give up on trying
to train him.      5 4 3 2 1 0

s. My child continues to beg and plead to have his way
after I have denied his appeal the first time.      5 4 3 2 1 0

t. My child is more disobedient and disrespectful in front
of others than he is when he knows that such behavior
is not likely to embarrass me.      5 4 3 2 1 0

2. Based on your answers to the manipulation test, what emotional
responses do you find yourself having most often? (Guilt, shame,
embarrassment, hurt, anger, impatience)

3. Which (if any) of the wrong parental reactions do you find yourself
using in response to manipulation? (Defending, justifying, blame shift-
ing, answering "why" questions, yelling, giving up)

# Chapter 10
## Study Questions

1. List five guidelines which help when responding to manipulation.

2. What should one's motive be when responding to manipulation?

3. Of what does Galatians, chapter six, warn we should be careful when attempting to restore someone who is sinning?

4. When you are angry, what might alert you that your anger is sinful, not righteous?

5. For each of the following examples, write out what the parent could have said and/or done instead.

Child:   "You never let me go out with my friends."
Parent:

Child:   "May I have something to eat?"
Parent:  "Not now."
Child:   "But, I'm hungry."
Parent:

Child:   "May I go over to my friend's house?"
Parent:  "No. You have homework to do."
Child:   (whining) "Why can't I do my homework later?"
Parent:

Child:   "Can I watch TV?"
Parent:  "You know the rule; no TV until homework is done and dinner is over."
Child:   "Please."
Parent:  "No."
Child:   "Just this once?"
Parent:

# Chapter 10
# Application Questions

1. Of the angry forms of communication listed in this chapter, are there some with which you particularly struggle? If yes, which ones? If yes, what specific changes do you need to make?

2. Keep a manipulation journal for the next two weeks. Summarize what observations you have made or things you have learned by doing this.

3. After reading this chapter and the previous one, have you discovered any ways in which you have been guilty of manipulating others? What are your favorite manipulative techniques?

## Elements of Manipulative Behavior

| The Behavior | Desired Emotional Response | Parental Reaction | Desired Controlling Effect | Sinful Motives |
|---|---|---|---|---|
| Accusations | Guilt | Defend self | To procrastinate | Love of pleasure |
| Criticisms | Shame | Justify actions | To avoid obligation | Love of power |
| Crying | Embarrassment | Blame shifting | To change parent's mind | Love of praise |
| "Why" questions | Hurt | Answer "why" questions | To lower parents' standard | Love of money |
| Obligatory Statements | Anger | Yelling back | To rescind parental punishment | Love of (anything)... |
| Sulking, Pouting | | | | food, safety, no homework, comfort, toys, freedom, a car, etc... |
| Whining | | | | |
| Withholding affection | | | | |
| Cold shoulder | | | | (see Appendix C. for additional motives) |

# Chapter 11
## Study Questions

1. Explain what a think room is *not*.

2. Explain what a think room *is*.

3. How can a Christian parent use a think room?

# Chapter 11
## Application Questions

1. How could you use (or how are you already using) a think room in your home?

2. What room or area of your home is best suited for a think room?

3. What resources will you place there for your children to utilize?

# Chapter 12
## Study Questions

1. Write out how a child who wants to go fishing with a friend on Saturday morning can properly appeal to his parents when the house rule is that chores are to be done on Saturday morning.

2. Can children appeal all rules?

3. Write out the steps in making a biblical appeal.

4. How is it manipulation to make an appeal to the parent who *did not* give the instruction?

5. When might children lose the appeal privilege?

6. Explain specifically how a child should be taught to respond when an appeal is denied.

# Chapter 12
# Application Questions

1. Give an example of a time when you made an appeal. Did your appeal follow the guidelines listed in this chapter? If not, where did your appeal deviate from these guidelines?

2. If your children do not know how to make a biblical appeal, teach them how to do so. Write out an example of how one of your children used the appeal process.

# Chapter 13
# Study Questions

1. What might be the problem if you find you are not able to fulfill your biblical responsibilities as a parent?

2. What may be the problem if you are not seeing your children respond?

3. What will happen if you persevere in this area?

# Chapter 13
# Application Questions

1. What are the principles that most stand out to you from this book?

2. Are there principles from this book you want to put into use and continue to use in your daily life? Is so, what are they?

3. Are there specific ways this book has helped you to grow as a parent? If so, how?

4. Are there specific ways this book has helped you to grow in your relationship with Jesus Christ? If so, how?

## Appendix
# Extra Journals and Worksheets

The remaining pages of this workbook contain additional copies of the Anger Journal, the Heart Journal, the Conflict Journal, and the Anti-manipulation Worksheet. These are provided for you to photocopy and use when and where necessary.

# Anger Journal

*1. What circumstances led to my becoming angry?*
*(What happened to provoke my anger?*

_____

_____

_____

_____

_____

*2. What did I say/do when I became angry?*
*(How did I respond to the circumstances?)*

_____

_____

_____

_____

_____

*3. What is the biblical evaluation of what I said/did when I became angry?*
*(How does the Bible classify what I said/did when I became angry?)*

_____

_____

_____

_____

_____

*4. What should I have said/done when I became angry?*
*(How could I have responded biblically when I became angry?)*

_____

_____

_____

_____

_____

# Heart Journal

*1. What happened to provoke me to anger?*
*(What were the circumstances that led to my becoming angry?)*

_____

_____

_____

_____

_____

*2. What did I say to myself (in my heart) when I became angry?*
*(What did I want, desire, or long for when I became angry?)*

_____

_____

_____

_____

_____

*3. What does the Bible say about what I said to myself when I became angry?*
*(What does the bible say about what I wanted?)*

_____

_____

_____

_____

_____

*4. What should I have said to myself when I became angry? (What should I*
*have wanted more than my own selfish and idolatrous desire?)*

_____

_____

_____

_____

_____

# Conflict Journal

*Circumstances surrounding the conflict:*

_____

_____

_____

_____

_____

*Parent:* _____

*Child:* _____

*Parent:* _____

*Child:* _____

*Parent:* _____

*Child:* _____

*Parent:* _____

*Child:* _____

*Parent:* _____

*Child:* _____

# Antimanipulation Worksheet

*Circumstances surrounding manipulation:*

_____

_____

_____

_____

_____

*Manipulative remarks made to me:*

_____

_____

_____

_____

_____

*My response to the manipulation:*

_____

_____

_____

_____

_____

*Christlike (biblical) response to the manipulation:*

_____

_____

_____

_____

_____